Written by
Lacie Brueckner & Katherine Pendergast

In Loving Memory

A Child's Journey to Understanding a Funeral and Starting the Grieving Process

Illustrated by
Svetlana Kuznetsova

Written by Lacie Brueckner and Katherine Pendergast.
Illustrated by Svetlana Kuznetsova. Layout by Anna Brutman.
Text, layout, and illustrations copyright © 2020 by Kat's Socks.
All rights reserved.

Published by Kat's Socks.
Bismarck, ND, USA.
Printed and bound in China.

Download your free healthy grieving idea
worksheet at www.katssocks.com/pages/grieving
katssocks.com

Library of Congress Control Number: 2020906529
ISBN 978-1-7340750-2-1

I have lost someone special to me.
Their name is _____ .

Place a picture
of you together here

Early one morning, Harper awoke to a loving hand on her shoulder.

"Harper, do you remember when we learned that plants, animals, and people live and die?" asked her mom. Harper nodded.

"Well, I have something important to tell you," her mom said. "Grandma passed away last night. I want you to know she loved you very much, Harper. She will always be in our hearts, and now she is in heaven with Grandpa."

Harper pressed her face to her mom's chest and cried. What now? she wondered.

The next day, Harper said, "Mom, I'm sad. I miss Grandma."

"Feeling sad, angry, or frightened is part of the grieving process. Maybe we can do something that Grandma enjoyed," her mom suggested. "What are some of your favorite memories with Grandma?"

Harper thought about all of her favorite memories. "I loved playing card games with Grandma!"

"I loved baking cookies with Grandma," she told her mom. "Monster cookies were her favorite."

Harper's mother hugged her. "I think we have all the ingredients for monster cookies," she said into Harper's ear. "How about we make those? I miss Grandma too. I'm glad we can do things together that remind us of her."

A few days later, Harper and her family drove to a strange building. A sign out front read, "Funeral Home."

"Would you like to see Grandma now?" Harper's mom asked when they went inside.

Harper nodded. "Yes, I do want to see her."

"Okay," said her mom, "but remember, she is not alive. Her body might look a little different from what you remember. When we die, our bodies go through natural changes."

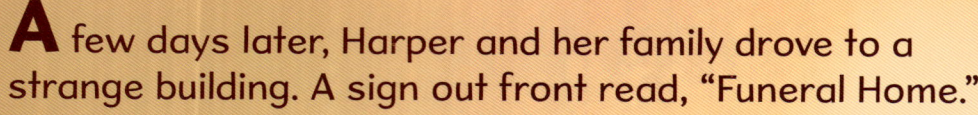

That evening, Harper and her family gathered to honor her grandma. Her mom called it a visitation.

"Some people will get up and talk about their favorite memories of Grandma," said Harper's mom. "Do you want to share a memory you had with Grandma?"

After a moment, Harper nodded, and then walked to the front of the room.

For a while, Harper stood silently. "My favorite memory of Grandma," she slowly began, "was going on vacation to Florida. I loved going to the beach and collecting seashells with her."

That night, Harper dreamed of finding her grandma's favorite seashell and watching her grandma smile.

The next day, they arrived at Grandma's church. Harper held her mom's hand as they walked to their seats.

"Today is the funeral," said her mom, squeezing Harper's fingers tight. "We will have a celebration of life service."

Afterward, they headed to the cemetery. "This is where Grandma will be laid for her final resting spot," her mom explained. "A place we can return to anytime you feel like visiting Grandma."

"Now that Grandma's burial is over, we can head back to the church for lunch and enjoy some of Grandma's famous monster cookies that we made," Harper's mom said.

"Look at the beautiful flowers on the tables. They were Grandma's favorite."

Weeks passed. Then months.

"Harper, did you know today was Grandma's birthday?" her mom asked one day. "She would have been seventy-six years old."

"Wow," Harper exclaimed. "I sure miss Grandma."

"Sometimes special events like holidays and birthdays bring up feelings of missing Grandma. How about we do something special today? We could find some purple flowers and take them out to the cemetery." suggested her mom. "You know purple was her favorite color."

Harper smiled. "I would love that. Let's go."

The next day, Harper walked into the kitchen.

"What are you working on, Mom?" asked Harper.

"I was thinking about your grandma," her mom began, "and I wanted to create a photo album about all of her favorite things. Would you like to help me?"

"Yes, I would love that." Harper flipped through the pictures in the album.

"There's Grandma's favorite dog, Dixie." Harper flipped to another page. "And there are her favorite purple flowers and her favorite monster cookies." She turned to the final page and saw a picture of herself.

"What's this?" Harper asked her mom.

Harper's mom hugged her hard. "Grandma's absolute favorite thing."

My favorite memory of _____ is

Write or draw

Harper does special activities that remind her of her grandma. What are some activities you can do to remember your loved one?

Write or draw

Lacie Brueckner

Lacie has been a funeral director serving families since 2005. She takes a special interest in meeting the needs of children during the funeral process, as they very much want and need to feel included too. In her experience she has found that including them and letting them lead the way in how much they want to be included usually works the best.

Lacie is a North Dakota native and lives there with her husband and five children. She has always had an interest in writing and was honored to coauthor this book.

Katherine Pendergast

Katherine lost her mom many years ago, and one of her favorite memories of her mom was on her last Mother's Day. They planted petunias and went out for ice cream. Now, every Mother's Day, Katherine plants petunias at her house not because they are her favorite but because they remind her of this special memory with her mom.

Katherine lives with her family and two dogs in Bismarck, North Dakota. She has also written several other books including her award-winning books **Pickles the Dog: Adopted, Pickles the Dog: A Christmas Tradition,** and **Babies of the Badlands.**